Quips
&
Quirks

Books by Clyde and Wendy Watson
FATHER FOX'S PENNYRHYMES
TOM FOX AND THE APPLE PIE
QUIPS & QUIRKS

Quips & Quirks

BY CLYDE WATSON

ILLUSTRATED BY
WENDY WATSON

THOMAS Y. CROWELL COMPANY
NEW YORK

Published simultaneously in Canada by
Fitzhenry & Whiteside Limited, Toronto.
Designed by Wendy Watson
Manufactured in the United States of America

LIBRARY OF CONGRESS
CATALOGING IN PUBLICATION DATA
Watson, Clyde.   Quips & quirks.
Bibliography: p.   Includes index.
SUMMARY: *Briefly defines a number of names used
to tease or insult for a hundred years or more. In-
cludes rubberneck, flibbertigibbet, trollybags, and
many more.   1. Epithets . . . Juv. lit.   [1. Epi-
thets]*
I. *Watson, Wendy, ill.*   II. *Title.*
PE*1447.W3*   *828'.02*   *75-4678*
ISBN *0-690-00733-7*

1 2 3 4 5 6 7 8 9 10

*F*or the original Ragabash Bear,
Crumbs in his Beard & all

CONTENTS

PREFACE

People have been calling each other names for centuries. Amused or annoyed by the looks, habits, and characters of their fellows, they have invented names to use both in fun and in earnest, to tease and to insult. No one is perfect: Some of us are greedy, some are grouchy, others are nosy or rude. There are names to fit us all, and so to express all the quips and quirks of human nature.

This book is a collection of such names. Most of them are at least one hundred years old, and some are quite a bit older. Though most names were probably hissed and hollered long before anyone wrote them down, we do know, from reading ancient books and manuscripts, that people have been calling each others FOOLS since the year 1275, HOGS since 1436, and STINKERS since 1600, if not longer.

I found these names during months of digging in old books and dictionaries. When I finally stopped dusting off words, I had gathered more than a thousand of them, and there must be plenty that I missed. I realized that I couldn't use so many words or my book would be too enormous. This is how I decided which names to keep:

1) Only one-word names could stay. (I sadly kissed KEYHOLE KATE and CAPTAIN QUEERNABS good-bye.)

2) Where six or seven names in one category contained the same word, I chose the name I liked best, and threw out the rest. For example, for GLUTTONS I had a choice of greedy-devil, greedy-eater, greedy-glutton, greedy-grabs, greedy-guts, greedy-hog, and greedy-muffin. I chose greedy-grabs.

3) If a word didn't have a certain ring to it—rhythm, pep, and a sense of humor—out it went.

What is left is a pocketful of plums, the pick of the bunch. There are many more where these came from, and if you hunt patiently you will certainly find some. The bibliography at the end of this book suggests some places to start looking.

Clyde Watson
Lyme, New Hampshire
September 1974

Quips
&
Quirks

Pepperpot is in a Frenzy
Everyone watch out!
She's spitting Flames & spewing Smoke
The nasty-tempered Lout

Fire engines, to the Rescue
Roaring through the Town
Pour on Water quick & cold
To cool the Hot-head down

HOTHEADS

BRIMSTONE & PEPPERPOT have hasty Tempers[1]

FIRE-EATER looks for Quarrels & Disturbance

HOT-SPUR is a fierce, furious Fellow

MADBRAIN is a bad-tempered Hot-head

MAKE-BATE starts Squabbles & picks Fights[2]

SPITFIRE spews Flames in angry Fits

TINDERBOX is ready to flare up at the least Provocation[3]

WAXPOT is quick to fly into a Rage[4]

1. BRIMSTONE *is an old name for sulfur, a mineral which catches fire easily. Brimstone is used in making matches, fireworks, and gunpowder.*

2. BATE *used to mean quarrels or strife.*
3. *A* TINDERBOX *held* TINDER—*any material like dry paper or scorched linen which catches fire easily. Usually the box also held a flint and a piece of steel to strike a spark to light the tinder to start a fire.*
4. *A* WAX *is an angry feeling or a fit of rage.*

1

PESTS, *who are always hang-ing around where they are not wanted, getting in the Way & making themselves Obnoxious:*

BRAT
BOTHERATION
NETTLE[1]
NUISANCE
PAIN
PEST
PLAGUE[2]

1. A NETTLE *is a plant with tiny prickly hairs which make your skin sting and burn if you touch them.*
2. To PLAGUE *means to tease or torment.*

SISSIES

CREAMPUFF is as soft & fragile as a Creampuff Pastry

FANCY-PANTS won't dirty his pretty Clothes, nor his tender Hands

HEN-HEART runs at the least Hint of Danger

JELLY-FISH is a weak, spineless Creature

MILKSOP is a feeble Fellow easily controlled

MOLLYCODDLE treats himself like a precious Infant & expects others to do the same

SISSY acts very delicate & babyish

SOFTY is a spoiled Weakling

TENDERLING is a dainty, pampered Darling

YELLOW-BELLY is a sorry, chicken-hearted Coward

3

COMPLAINERS

BELLYACHER whines & complains loudly

CRUSTY-GRIPES is always to be heard grumbling & grousing[1]

FUSSBUDGET is never satisfied with Anything the way it is

GRIZZLEGUTS mopes & moans about[2]

PILGARLIC feels sorry for himself & wants others to do likewise[3]

SOURBALL never stops muttering about how Bad it all is

SQUAWKER is sure to holler when Things aren't to his Liking

1. CRUSTY *means peevish or snappish; a* GRIPE *is a complaint.*
2. *In Britain, to* GRIZZLE *means to fret, whine, or complain tearfully.*

3. *The name* PILGARLIC *(or peeled garlic) was first used to poke fun at a man with a bald head. Later it came to mean "poor creature," and when someone called himself "Poor Pilgarlic" he meant "Poor Me."*

Bellyache, Bellyache
Loud & Long
Leave it up to Fusspot
To find Something Wrong

CHEEKERS

BRASSFACE is pert & bold as Brass

CHEEKER is apt to talk back, a fresh cocky Thing[1]

JACKSAUCE is rude & saucy

RUDESBY is insolent & unruly

SAUCEBOX behaves with sassy Manners

WISECRACKER cracks Jokes to poke Fun at others

1. CHEEK *means insolence, freshness.*

NOBODIES

DANDIPRAT is a small Fellow of no account, not worth Two Cents[1]

FOPDOODLE is a conceited Nobody

JACKSTRAW is a mere Puppet, a Man of Straw

PIPSQUEAK is a useless little Runt

SNIPJACK is a worthless Creature

SPRAT is beneath Notice, a little Fish[2]

SQUIRT acts Big but amounts to Little

WHIFFET is a Bit of Nothing, a Whiff of Air

WHISK puts on Airs, a rude, puny Fellow

1. In sixteenth-century England a DANDIPRAT was a small silver coin worth three half-pence—not much.

2. A SPRAT is a certain small fish, also a small English coin.

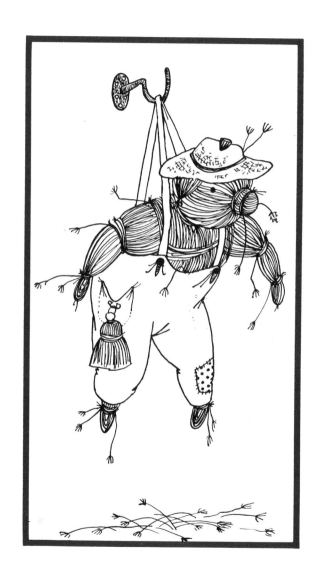

7

*R*ed-Rag, Lollygag
Open those sweet brown Eyes
If you're not up by the Count of three
You're in for a rude Surprise

Red-Rag, Lollygag
Now the time has come
So off with the Covers & let you lie bare
And shiver, you lazy Bum!

LAZY BUMS

BUM is an idle Good-for-Nothing
DO-NOTHING does Naught & is
    worth Naught
IDLEBACK lollygags around doing
    Nothing
LAZYBONES was born lazy
LOAFER lounges & lazes, watching
    others work
LOLLPOOP leans lazily out the
    Window & even puts out his
    Tongue at those who pass by[1]

LOOBY is a lazy, hulking Oaf
POKE-EASY moves in a slow, lazy
    Way & dawdles over his Work[2]
SLUGABED spends the best Part
    of each Day lying in Bed
TELL-CLOCK lies about watching
    Time pass[3]

1. *To* LOLL *means to lean or rest lazily against something.*

2. *To* POKE *means to work or move about slowly, lazily, and ineffectively.*
3. TELL *once meant to count. We still use this old sense of the word when we talk about "telling time." A* TELLCLOCK *counts the hours on the* CLOCK.

BOORS, *rough, ignorant Creatures unacquainted with the finer Things of life, more comical than offensive with their ill-bred, clumsy Manners:*

BOOR[1]
BUMPKIN
CHURL[2]
CLODHOPPER[3]
CLUNCH
HAYSEED
HICK

HOBNAIL[4]
LOBLOLLY[5]
LOUT
LUMPKIN
WHOPSTRAW[6]
YOKEL

1. *The Dutch word* BOER *means farmer or peasant.*
2. *In Angle-Saxon times a* CEORL *was a freeman of the lowest rank—a common man.*
3. *A* CLOD *is a lump of earth.*

4. HOBNAILS *are short, sharp nails used as studs for the kind of sturdy shoes or boots a farmer might wear.*
5. LOBLOLLY *is a thick gruel often spoken of as country food.*
6. WHOP *means to make straw into bundles.*

SPOILSPORTS

ADDLEPLOT wrecks everything by butting in or acting up[1]

CRAPEHANGER brings a gloomy Air to any Gathering[2]

KILLJOY takes the Fun out of Things with his dismal Remarks

SPOILSPORT ruins Games, especially when he's losing

TROUBLEMIRTH spoils Good Cheer & Merrymaking[3]

WETBLANKET dampens High Spirits like Water puts out Fire

1. *To* ADDLE *means to rot or go bad; a* PLOT *is a plan.*
2. CRAPE *is a kind of thin black cloth used to make funeral clothes and to* HANG *in windows as a sign of mourning.*
3. MIRTH *is happiness and laughter.*

*V*inegar, *Vinegar, cranky & cross*
Sit in the Corner & pout
Plug your Ears & shut your Eyes
And stick your red Tongue out

CRANKS

CRABSTICK is grouchy & ill-natured[1]
CRANK is sour & snappish
CROSSPATCH is sullen & bad-tempered
GLUMP pouts & sulks

MOLLYGRUBS is cross & cranky[2]
PICKLEPUSS is glum & unpleasant
RUSTYGUTS is surly & blunt[3]
SOURBELLY is morose & crabby
SOREHEAD is huffy & disgruntled
VINEGAR scowls & frowns
WORRY-CARL is snarling & mean-tempered

1. *A* CRABSTICK *is a* STICK *of wood from a crab apple tree. The tree is gnarled and rough, its fruit bitter and harsh, just like the temper of a* CRABBY *person.*

2. MOLLYGRUBS *is an old word for colic: pains in the stomach which can make a person very grumpy.*
3. RUSTY *means cross, nasty, or ill-tempered in British dialect.*

NOSYBODIES

BUSYBODY noses rudely about in Other People's Business & can't resist giving his Two Cents' Worth

EAVESDROPPER sneaks around secretly listening in on private Conversations[1]

GONGOOZLER stands idly gaping at Anything unusual

QUIDNUNC is an inquisitive Creature apt to gossip[2]

RUBBERNECK twists his Neck & turns his Head to stare in Curiosity

STICKY-BEAK must poke his Neb into everyone else's Affairs[3]

1. *The strip of ground alongside a house where rainwater drips down from the eaves was called the eavesdrip or* EAVESDROP. *A person who stood within the eavesdrop could listen through walls, windows, and doors to what was said inside.*

2. QUID NUNC? *means "What now?" in Latin. Nosy people always ask eagerly, "What now? What's the latest?"*

3. *In Australia, the* STICKY-BEAK *is a bird that gets its* BEAK STICKY *searching for food.*

I know a nasty Nebnose
Who's very rude & sly
She goes about on Tiptoes
To eavesdrop & to pry

She digs through People's Wastebaskets
To see what she can find
She even reads their private Mail
A Habit most unkind

When she thinks the Coast is clear
She gets down on All Fours
To peek through People's Keyholes
And listen at their Doors

This Person has no Manners
And you can plainly see
That delving into others' Lives
Is quite her Specialty

STINKERS, *those Persons who are repulsive, loathsome, scorned . . . in short, generally objectionable and therefore disliked:*

CREEP
CROCK
CRUMB
DRIP
FISH-FACE
HUMGRUFFIN
MULLIPUFF
PILL
RATBAG
ROTTER
RUNT
SHEEP-GUTS
STINKPOT
TWERP

FUDDY-DUDDIES

BACK-NUMBER is a dusty, outdated Person[1]

DODO is stupidly behind the Times[2]

FOGY is against Anything new or different

FOSSIL is full of old-fashioned Ideas & is not in tune with the Present[3]

HAS-BEEN has had his Day & lives in the Past

MOSSBACK doesn't move with the Times, but sits unchanging, like a Stone growing a Cover of Moss

SQUARE-TOES is a terribly old-fashioned Fusspot[4]

STICK-IN-THE-MUD is a poky old Fogy

1. *Old issues of magazines are called* BACK-NUMBERS.

2. *There once lived a bird called a* DODO *(which comes from the Portuguese word* DOUDO, *meaning "stupid" or "silly"). It had a huge, clumsy body and small wings and could not fly. The dodo is now extinct.*

3. FOSSILS *are the remains of plants and animals belonging to past ages, found imbedded in layers of the earth's surface.*

4. *At one time,* SQUARE-TOED *shoes were considered old-fashioned, pointed ones up-to-date.*

CHATTERBOXES

CHATTERBASKET keeps up a steady Hum of idle Babbling

FLAPJAW never gives his Jaw a Rest, nor his Listener's Ears

JABBERMOUTH cackles & gabbles like a Goose

JACKDAW is a noisy Nuisance[1]

MAGPIE chatters & scolds Day In & Day Out[2]

PRATE-ROAST jabbers & prattles endlessly[3]

RATTLETRAP is a silly Chatterbag

WINDJAMMER is a great windy Talker

TONGUE-PAD talks too much[4]

1. *A* JACKDAW *is a loudmouthed bird.*
2. *A* MAGPIE *is another noisy bird.*

3. *To* PRATE *means to chatter or babble.*
4. *To* PAD *means to travel or walk; a* TONGUE-PAD *is one whose* TONGUE *travels at high speed.*

Yip-yap Rattletrap
Prating noisy Pest
Stuff a Muffin in your Mouth
And let my poor Ears rest!

HAREBRAINS

ADDLEPATE is full of Fancies &
   Ideas but too muddled to act on
   them
FEATHERHEAD is giddy & light-
   headed
PUZZLEPATE   &   RATTLE-
   SKULL are bewildered by the
   simplest Notions
SCATTERBRAIN never can pay
   Attention, his Wits wander so

FATTIES

BLUBBER-BELLY wears an extra
    Layer of Fat around his Middle
DUMPLING is a roly-poly Pud-
    ding, a Butterball
FATSO is also known as "Fats" or
    "Fattie"
JELLY-BELLY has a fat, wobbly
    Stomach
POTBELLY sticks out at the Waist
    like a Cook Kettle
PUFF-GUTS looks like a blown-up
    Balloon
SWAGBELLY is known by his
    projecting Paunch[1]
TUBS is round as a Tub

1. SWAG *is an old word for a bulging bag.*

21

In frayed & frazzled Rags & Jags
Comes sloppy, slovenly Trollybags
All ripped & raggedy
Saggy baggedy
Rumpled & ruffled & Hair all shaggedy
Sloppy, slovenly Trollybags
In frayed & frazzled Rags & Jags

SLOBS

DISHCLOUT is a gray & grimy Creature, a Dishrag[1]

FUSTILUGS is a filthy, overgrown Slob[2]

MALKINTRASH is a frightful Sight, dressed like a Scarecrow[3]

RAGABASH wears mean, shabby Clothes

SHAGRAG neither combs his Hair nor mends his Britches

SLOVEN lives like a Pig with lazy, filthy Habits

SLUBBERDEGULLION is a nasty slobbering Lout

TATTERWALLOP goes about in torn & tattered Rags

TROLLYBAGS is repulsive & dirty[4]

1. *In British dialect, a* CLOUT *is a rag or cloth.*
2. FUSTY *means dirty; in Scottish dialect,* LUGS *are ears.*
3. *In British dialect,* MALKIN *is a scarecrow, a ragged puppet.*

4. *In North English dialect,* TROLLYBAGS *means "sheep-guts."*

NUMSKULLS, *or such Persons as appear to have either hollow Heads, empty of Brains; solid Heads, with no Room for Brains; or dull Heads, with tiny Brains:*

BIRDBRAIN
BLOCKHEAD
BONEHEAD
CHUMP
CLODPOLL[1]
DIMWIT
DOLT
DULLDICK
DUMB-BELL

DUNCE[2]
DUNDERPATE
FATHEAD
HALFWIT
IMBECILE[3]
MORON[4]

2. *The* DUNCE, *in Colonial schools, was the student who didn't learn his lessons, and for punishment had to sit on the dunce block wearing a dunce's peaked cap.*
3. *The Latin word* IMBECILLUS *means weak or feeble.*
4. *The Greek word* MORON *means sluggish, dull, stupid.*

1. CLOD *means lump,* POLL *means head.*

NUMSKULL
PEABRAIN
SHALLOWBRAINS
SOFTHEAD
THICKWIT
TOMNODDY[5]

5. A NODDY *is a fool or simpleton.*

Beware the idle whispering Gossip
Pricking up her Ears
Tittle-tattle goes her Tongue
Repeating what she hears

DON'T TELL ANYONE BUT YOU'LL NEVER GUESS WELL JUST BETWEEN YOU AND ME OF ALL THINGS I DECLARE WELL I'LL BE GRACIOUS INDEED CAN YOU BEAT THAT YOU WON'T BELIEVE DID YOU KNOW WHAT'S THE WORLD COMING TO WHAT'S THE WORLD COMING

WAY DON'T TELL ANYONE BUT INDEED WELL I'LL BE YOU WON'T BELIEVE JUST BETWEEN YOU AND ME OF ALL THINGS I DECLARE CAN YOU BEAT THAT WELL GRACIOUS YOU'LL NEVER GUESS WHAT'S THE WORLD COMING DID YOU KNOW A FINE HOW-DEE-DO

26

GOSSIPS

BLABBERMOUTH cannot keep his Mouth shut but tells All he knows

FLIBBERTIGIBBET loves Nothing so well as Tea & Gossip

GOSSIP runs from House to House tattling & telling News[1]

NEWSMONGER collects & spreads Rumors & Hearsay[2]

POLL-PARROT repeats Everything he hears

TATTLETALE is a whispering Talebearer

WAGTONGUE chatters with a mean Tongue that is "hinged in the Middle & wags at both Ends"

1. GOSSIPS *were the godmothers and godfathers at a baptism. Before and after the ceremony no doubt they would chat and exchange news—or* GOSSIP.

2. *A* MONGER *is a peddler.*

SKINNIES, *who are known by many Names:*

BEAN-POLE
BROOMSTICK
DRAINPIPE
GANGLESHANKS[1]
HAIRPIN
MATCHSTICK
PIPECLEANER
RACKABONES
RAZORBLADE
RIBSKIN
SKINNYBONES
SPARERIBS
SPINDLESHANKS[2]
STRINGBEAN
TINRIBS

1. GANGLY *means spindly or awkward;* SHANKS *are legs.*
2. *A* SPINDLE *is a thin wooden stick tapering at both ends, used to* SPIN *flax or wool.*

KNOW-ALLS

IGNORAMUS plays the Scholar, peppering his Speech with Latin words and making a Fool of himself in the process[1]

KNOW-IT-ALL acts as if he knows Everything under the Sun

SMARTALECK shows off his so-called Knowledge at every Chance

WISEACRE pretends Great Wisdom but is woefully ignorant

WITLING thinks himself very clever with his poor Puns & sorry Jokes

1. IGNORAMUS *means "we are ignorant" in Latin.*

29

GLUTTONS

BELLY-GOD worships his Belly

GLUTTON eats too much too fast

GOBBLE-GUT chokes down his Meals

GREEDY-GRABS never waits for Grace but grabs what's nearest & starts to eat

POKE-PUDDING is a round-faced Gundigut[1]

SLAPSAUCE is a greedy Glutton fond of fine Food

SLOBBERCHOPS is a great loud slobbering Hog[2]

SLUSHBUCKET eats noisily & has no Manners

SWILLBELLY guzzles & slurps like a Pig[3]

---

1. POKE-PUDDING *is cooked in a* POKE *or bag. The glutton who eats too much poke-pudding starts to look like one.*

2. CHOPS *means mouth and jaws (as in "licking his chops").*

3. SWILL *is what the farmer feeds his pig.*

Here sits Master Greedy-Guts
His Face stuffed full of Food
The Overflow runs down his Chin
His Manners are quite crude

He gobbles down nice dainty Things
The way a Pig eats Slops
He slurps his Soup & smacks his Lips
And licks his greasy Chops

Whatever's set upon the Table
Must go down his Throat
Or end up squashed beneath his Feet
And splattered on his Coat

Heaps & Hills of Mashed Potato
Platters full of Pork
Great huge Gobs of Raisin Pudding
Balanced on his Fork

A sorry Sight! he eats & eats
Until he's almost ill
Then tops it off with one more Swig:
At last he's had his Fill

WINDBAGS

BAGPIPE talks a lot but says Little

BLATHERSKITE speaks pure Nonsense[1]

GASBAG is full of Hot Air & empty Talk

PIFFLER spouts feeble, foolish Falderol

TWADDLER pours forth Fudge & Flapdoodle

WINDBAG makes more Noise than Sense

WHIFFLER is a trivial, idle Prater

1. To BLETHER *(or* BLATHER*) means to talk stupidly; and in dialect a* SKITE *is a disagreeable person.*

NITWITS, *silly Fools who, judging by their Behavior, lack all Sense & Intelligence:*

BOOBY
CALF-LOLLY
CONY[1]
DAWKIN
FOOL
GOOSECAP
IDIOT
JOBBERNOWL
NICK-NINNY
NIGMENOG

NINCOMPOOP
NINNYHAMMER
NODDY
NOODLE
OAF
PEAGOOSE[2]
PATCH
SIMPLETON
TOMFOOL

1. CONY *is an old word for rabbit.*

2. PEAGOOSE *is a combination of* PEAK, *an old word for simpleton, and* GOOSE.

CRYBABIES

BAWLBABY starts howling at the slightest little Thing

BLUBBERMOUTH is a noisy, slobbering Crybaby

CRYBABY cries as easily & as often as an Infant

WATERWORKS can turn his Tears off & on like a Faucet

C – R – Y – B – A – B – Y

Blubberbaby's going to cry
He'll stop howling by & by
When the Waterworks run dry

Cheapskate, Hide your Plate
There's Company at the Door
Give them a Seat, but Nothing to eat
Or they'll only ask for More

Cheapskate, Fetch your Plate
Your Guests have said Good-bye
Fill up your Cup, and now you may sup
On cold Potato Pie

36

MISERS

CHEAPSKATE spends as little as possible, even when treating his Friends

CLUTCHFIST never lets go of his precious Purse

CURMUDGEON is a greedy, grasping Pennypincher

LOVE-PENNY hoards Coins & gloats over them

MISER hides away his Money & lives Miserably

MONEYBAGS loves Riches

MUCKTHRIFT is a moneygrubbing Miser[1]

NIPCHEESE is pinching & close-fisted

PINCHGUT starves himself & others

SCRAT & SCRIMP make do with Scraps rather than part with Cash

SKINFLINT is a mean, stingy Fellow

TIGHTWAD is never generous but keeps a tight Hold on his Wad of Bills

1. MUCK means dirt or manure, but it is also a scornful name for money. THRIFT is the careful management of money.

DONKEYS

BITTERENDER will not compromise or give in, but sticks firm to the Finish

DIE-HARD keeps fighting a new Rule long after Everyone Else has accepted it

MULE stands stubbornly with both Feet braced

PIGHEAD is stupidly obstinate

STANDPAT won't budge from his own Point of View

STICKLER argues picky Points

STIFFNECK will not bend or give an Inch

NUTS, *including those who are odd or slightly "off" as well as those who are stark, raving mad:*

CRACKBRAIN
CUCKOO[1]
LUNATIC
MADCAP
MAGGOT[2]
MANIAC
ODDBALL
SCREWLOOSE

1. *The* CUCKOO *is a bird that repeats the same monotonous call over and over. It also has a strange habit of laying its eggs in other birds' nests instead of in its own.*
2. *People used to believe that a person who acted strange or crazy had* MAGGOTS *in his head eating away at his brains.*

*H*ere comes Captain Cockalorum
Finest of the Fine
A puffed-up, proud & pompous Fool
He's on his way to Dine

In green silk Shirt & velvet Pants
And sweetly perfumed Hair
See how he swaggers, bows & struts
With Nose up in the Air

Alas for him he does not see
The Puddle in his Path
A moment later, down he goes
Into a muddy Bath

In vain he waves his Arms & Legs
The Crowd roars at the Sight
The more he curses, kicks & shouts
The greater their Delight

40

SHOWOFFS

COCKALORUM is a very confident little Man

COXCOMB is foolishly proud of his Looks, Costume & Accomplishments[1]

FOP flaunts fashionable Clothes & fancy Manners

GIMCRACK puts on all sorts of Airs

JACKADANDY is a little cocky conceited Fellow[2]

PEACOCK parades & shows off Feathers & Finery

POWDERPUFF uses Creams, Powders & Lotions to make himself elegant

POPINJAY is a vain & light-headed Dandy[3]

PRINCOX is a saucy young Fop

PUFFIN is a pompous Fool, full of Self-Importance[4]

SWELLHEAD thinks himself a very Grand & Important Person

SWINGBREECH struts about in splendid Trousers[5]

TINHORN is a flashy Showoff as cheap & loud as a Tin Horn

WAGFEATHER boasts elegant Clothes & haughty Airs

WHIPPERSNAPPER is an arrogant little Upstart

1. *A* COXCOMB *was a fool's or court-jester's cap. It was the same shape and color as a* COCK'S, *or rooster's,* COMB.
2. *A* DANDY *is a person who gives great attention to his clothes.*

3. *A* POPINJAY *is a bright-colored, showy parrot.*
4. *A* PUFFIN *is a kind of sea-bird with a puffed-out chest.*
5. BREECHES *or britches are pants.*

CLUMSIES

BLUNDERBUSS is a stupid, clumsy Person[1]

BUTTERFINGERS drops Things all the Time

CLUTTERBUCK is always underfoot, the sleepyheaded Clown

FUMBLE-FIST is a clumsy-handed Bungler

GAMMERSTANG is tall & ungainly[2]

GAWK is an awkward Fool

GILLY-GAUPUS is a careless Creature, apt to break Things

LUMMOX is a big unwieldy Hulk, a "Bull in a China Closet"

1. Around 1690 a BLUNDERBUSS *was a heavy, unwieldy gun, hard to handle.*

2. GAMMER *was a country name for an old woman, and* STANG *meant pole. The name* GAMMERSTANG *described a woman as tall and gawky as a pole—but the name was used for men too.*

EXTRAS, *or a Hodgepodge of remarkable Characters:*

BUBBLE is a Sucker, one easily tricked & cheated

BULLYRAGGER upsets others by teasing & picking on them[1]

FIND-FAULT points at Other People's Faults instead of seeing to his own

FIZGIG & GADABOUT gaily shop, visit & gossip All Day[2]

1. In old slang the tongue was called the RED RAG; *to* RAG *someone means to torment him with the tongue, by teasing, scoffing, calling names, etc.*
2. To GAD *is to wander idly about.*

43

FLATTERCAP & SOFTSOAP will speak sweet Words & pretty Lies to get what they want

HEDGEHOG is a rude, selfish Thing careless of Other People's Feelings

HUFFSNUFF is a conceited, huffing Bully quick to take Offense

HUMDRUM is a dull, monotonous Bore

MUSHMOUTH mutters & mumbles his Words

PRIG says & does only what is perfectly Prim & Proper

SCATTERGOOD wastes what Next Day he wishes for

SHILLY-SHALLYER can never make up his Mind, and once he does, changes it[3]

SLOWPOKE is annoyingly slow & always behind

SMELLFEAST & LICKDISH will sniff out a Feast & show up uninvited, looking Hungry

SOBERSIDES never smiles but wears a stiff, serious Face[4]

WORRYWART frowns & worries over Nothing

3. *The shilly-shallyer, trying to make a decision, keeps asking "Shill I? Shall I?"*
4. SOBER *means grave or serious, straight-faced.*

BIBLIOGRAPHY

Any good dictionary will have quite a few names in it. Your librarian can probably suggest some books to look in, too. Here are some of the books I used in writing QUIPS & QUIRKS.

B. E. A NEW DICTIONARY . . . OF THE CANTING CREW. *London, 1798(?).*
This was the first slang dictionary ever printed. A few libraries still have copies of it in their rare-book rooms.

E. C. Brewer. DICTIONARY OF PHRASE AND FABLE. *London: Cassell & Co., 1870. New York: Harper & Row (rev. ed.), 1970.*
This delightful book is full of "Words that have a Tale to Tell," including many names.

Franklyn, Julian. A DICTIONARY OF NICK-NAMES. *London: Hamish Hamilton, 1962.*
Mostly British words.

THE OXFORD ENGLISH DICTIONARY. *New York: Oxford University Press, 1933.*
Most big libraries have the "O.E.D." in thirteen volumes, and now it is also available in two volumes of very small print, to be read with a magnifying glass. In it you can find out the earliest date a word is known to have existed, and there are lots of quotes from diaries, letters, novels, etc., to show how the word has been used.

Partridge, Eric. A DICTIONARY OF SLANG AND UNCONVENTIONAL ENGLISH. (1st ed.) *New York: The Macmillan Co., 1937.*
This book includes British, American, Australian, and Canadian names, old and new.

P. M. Roget. INTERNATIONAL THESAURUS. *3rd ed. New York: Thomas Y. Crowell Co., 1962.*
In this book you can look up any name and find a whole list of words with about the same meaning.

Wentworth, H., and Flexner, S. B. DICTIONARY OF AMERICAN SLANG. *New York: Thomas Y. Crowell Co., 1960.*
This book consists of recent and contemporary slang.

INDEX OF NAMES

49

quidnunc *14*

rackabones *28*
ragabash *23*
ratbag *16*
rattleskull *20*
rattletrap *18*
razorblade *28*
ribskin *28*
rotter *16*
rubberneck *14*
rudesby *6*
runt *16*
rustyguts *13*

saucebox *6*
scatterbrain *20*
scattergood *45*
scrat *37*
screwloose *39*
scrimp *37*
shagrag *23*
shallowbrains *25*
sheep-guts *16*
shilly-shallyer *45*
SHOWOFFS *41*
simpleton *33*
SISSIES *3*
skinflint *37*
SKINNIES *28*
skinnybones *28*
slapsauce *30*

slobberchops *30*
SLOBS *23*
sloven *23*
slowpoke *45*
slubberdegullion *23*
slugabed *9*
slushbucket *30*
smartaleck *29*
smellfeast *45*
snipjack *7*
sobersides *45*
softhead *25*
softsoap *44*
softy *3*
sorehead *13*
sourball *4*
sourbelly *13*
spareribs *28*
spindleshanks *28*
spitfire *1*
SPOILSPORTS *11*
sprat *7*
square-toes *17*
squawker *4*
squirt *7*
standpat *38*
stick-in-the-mud *17*
stickler *38*
sticky-beak *14*
stiffneck *38*
STINKERS *16*
stinkpot *16*

stringbean *28*
swagbelly *20*
swellhead *41*
swillbelly *30*
swingbreech *41*

tatterwallop *23*
tattletale *27*
tellclock *9*
tenderling *3*
thickwit *25*
tightwad *37*
tinderbox *1*
tinhorn *41*
tinribs *28*
tomfool *33*
tomnoddy *25*
tongue-pad *18*
trollybags *23*
troublemirth *11*
tubs *20*
twaddler *32*
twerp *16*

vinegar *13*

wagfeather *41*
wagtongue *27*
waterworks *34*
waxpot *1*
wetblanket *11*
whiffet *7*

whiffler *32*
whippersnapper *41*
whisk *7*
whopstraw *10*
WINDBAGS *32*
windjammer *18*
wiseacre *29*
wisecracker *6*
witling *29*
worry-carl *13*
worrywart *45*

yellow-belly *3*
yokel *10*

CLYDE and WENDY WATSON are sisters. They grew up in a large, lively, and creative family, nearly every member of which is a writer or an artist. Clyde is a graduate of Smith College and has taught in several schools, including one on an Indian reservation. She is an accomplished musician and composer, as well as a writer. Wendy, a graduate of Bryn Mawr College, has illustrated more than thirty books and has won many prizes and awards for her distinguished artwork. She is married and is the mother of a small child.

Besides QUIPS & QUIRKS, they have collaborated on several other books, including *Tom Fox and the Apple Pie* and *Father Fox's Penny-rhymes*. The latter was designated a Notable Book by the American Library Association, was runner-up for the National Book Award in 1972, and has established itself firmly as a modern American classic.